Mavin Murithi

WEALTH MAGNET: UNLOCKING KEY MONEY SECRETS FOR LOW-CAPITAL, HIGH-RETURN SUCCESS

First edition. September 14, 2023.

Copyright © 2023 Mavin Murithi.

ISBN: 979-8223067955

Written by Mavin Murithi.

Also by Mavin Murithi

Tall Confidence: Embrace Your Unique Journey to Self-Assuredness

Wealth Magnet: Unlocking Key Money Secrets for Low-Capital, High-Return Success

Wealth Magnet

Unlocking Key Money Secrets for Low-Capital, High-Return Success.

Chapter 9: Mastering Mindful Investing

- Navigating the World of Mindful Investing
- Defining Your Investment Goals and Intentions
- Embracing Risk and Building a Diversified Portfolio
- Conducting In-Depth Investment Research
- Balancing Patience and Action in Investing
- Exercises for Chapter 9

Chapter 10: Mapping Your Financial Future

- Crafting a Clear Vision for Financial Abundance
- Setting Specific and Achievable Milestones
- Designing Your Comprehensive Financial Plan
- Overcoming Obstacles and Challenges
- Regularly Reviewing and Adjusting Your Plan
- Exercises for Chapter 10

Conclusion: Your Path to Abundance

- Reflecting on Your Journey and Insights
- Crafting Personal Mantras for Success
- Setting Intentions and Sharing Your Vision
- Cultivating Gratitude and Embracing Continuous Learning
- Wrapping Up Your Financial Abundance Journey

Letter to the Reader
Contact Us
Recommended Resources
Glossary
Frequently Asked Questions

Acknowledgments

Writing "Wealth Magnet" has been a journey of growth, learning, and collaboration, and I am profoundly grateful for the individuals who have supported me along the way. Their encouragement, guidance, and inspiration have played an instrumental role in shaping this book and my perspective on financial empowerment.

First and foremost, I want to express my heartfelt gratitude to my family, whose unwavering support and belief in my vision have been my anchor throughout this endeavor. Your encouragement has fueled my determination to create a book that empowers readers to take control of their financial destinies.

I extend my deep appreciation to my mentors and advisors, whose wisdom and expertise have enriched the content of this book. Your insights have provided invaluable guidance in shaping the key money secrets and strategies shared within these pages.

To the remarkable individuals who shared their stories and experiences, thank you for allowing me to weave your journeys into the fabric of this book. Your contributions have added depth and relatability to the concepts discussed, enriching the reader's experience.

I am grateful to my dedicated team—editors, designers, and collaborators—who worked tirelessly to bring this book to life. Your passion and commitment to excellence have transformed my vision into reality.

A special thank you to every reader who embarks on this journey with "Wealth Magnet." Your openness to learning, growth, and empowerment inspires me. May the insights within these pages guide you to a life of abundance, purpose, and prosperity.

Lastly, I extend my heartfelt appreciation to the universe, which aligns opportunities and connections beyond our comprehension. Your guidance and the serendipitous moments that led to the creation of this book reaffirm my belief in the power of intention and manifestation.

With profound gratitude,

Mavin Murithi

Introduction: Unlocking Your Path to Financial Freedom

Welcome to the pages of "Wealth Magnet: Unlocking Key Money Secrets for Low-Capital, High-Return Success." If you've ever dreamed of gaining control over your financial destiny, this book is your guiding light toward that coveted realm of prosperity. In the following chapters, we will unravel the art of wealth creation through strategies that require minimal capital investment yet yield substantial returns. Prepare to embark on a journey that will reshape your perception of money, ignite your potential, and set you on a course to financial independence.

In a world that constantly whispers tales of financial limitations, it's time to redefine what's possible for you. This book isn't just about accumulating wealth; it's about harnessing the power of key money secrets to unlock the doors of opportunity that have been waiting for your touch. These secrets aren't guarded by dragons or hidden in labyrinthine caves; they are accessible and actionable insights that, when applied diligently, can bring about transformative change.

We believe that financial freedom isn't an elusive mirage reserved for the fortunate few; it's a destination that anyone can reach through knowledge, determination, and strategic action. Whether you're starting from scratch or seeking to amplify your existing resources, the principles you're about to discover will be your compass to navigate the vast landscape of wealth creation.

Our journey begins with embracing the cornerstone of success: the wealth mindset. Within these pages, you'll explore the profound impact that your beliefs and attitudes have on your financial reality. We'll delve into the psychology of wealth creation, unveiling the mental shifts necessary to attract abundance and seize opportunities.

From there, we'll traverse the terrain of skill monetization, uncovering the art of transforming your passions and talents into tangible income streams. We'll navigate the realm of passive income, where money works for you, freeing you from the confines of the traditional 9-to-5 grind. Digital entrepreneurship awaits, offering a world of online possibilities where creativity and innovation collide to yield remarkable returns.

But this journey isn't confined to virtual spaces; we'll also dive into real estate riches on a budget, demonstrating how calculated investments can yield substantial gains. Side hustles will become your allies in the pursuit of financial freedom, and frugality will reveal its potential to amplify your wealth-building efforts.

Networking, the art of cultivating valuable relationships, will empower you to harness the collective wisdom and opportunities that surround you. And through mindful investing, you'll demystify the world of financial markets, ensuring your hard-earned money is channeled into avenues that align with your goals.

Before you embark on this transformative journey, remember that every action begins with a decision. As you turn these pages, embrace the knowledge that you hold the power to steer your financial destiny. Let this book be your guide, your mentor, and your inspiration to seize the reins of your financial future.

Get ready to unlock your potential, embrace the principles of abundance, and let "Wealth Magnet" be the catalyst that propels you toward your aspirations. Your journey to financial freedom starts now.

Let's embark on this path together.

Warmest regards,

Mavin Murithi

Chapter 1: The Wealth Mindset

In the realm of financial empowerment, the journey begins not with bank accounts and investment portfolios, but with the most powerful asset of all—your mindset. The beliefs you hold about money, abundance, and your own potential set the stage for your financial reality. Welcome to the foundational chapter of "Wealth Magnet," where we explore the profound influence of the wealth mindset and unveil the keys to unlocking a world of prosperity.

The Psychology of Wealth Creation

Imagine your mind as a garden. Just as a well-tended garden yields abundant fruits, your thoughts and beliefs determine the harvest of your financial endeavors. The psychology of wealth creation is built on the understanding that your thoughts shape your reality. The seeds you plant in your mind can either flourish into a vibrant money tree or wither away into scarcity.

To cultivate a wealth mindset, start by acknowledging any limiting beliefs you may have about money. These beliefs might be inherited from childhood, societal conditioning, or past experiences. Challenge these beliefs by questioning their validity. Are they helping you grow or holding you back?

Shifting From Scarcity to Abundance

The shift from a scarcity mindset to an abundance mindset is pivotal. A scarcity mindset fixates on lack and limitation, often resulting in fear, anxiety, and missed opportunities. On the other hand, an abundance mindset focuses on the potential for growth, expansion, and possibilities. It invites gratitude for what you have and a genuine belief that more is attainable.

Begin this shift by practicing gratitude daily. Reflect on the things you're thankful for, no matter how small. This practice rewires your brain to focus on positives rather than dwelling on negatives.

Visualize Your Financial Success

Visualization is a potent tool used by successful individuals in various fields, including finance. Create a mental image of your desired financial success. Imagine living a life free of financial stress, pursuing your passions, and having the means to support your dreams. This visualization exercise sets a clear intention for your financial journey.

Cultivating Confidence and Self-Worth

Believing in your own worthiness of wealth is essential. Many individuals unconsciously block financial success due to feelings of unworthiness. Challenge this self-doubt by affirming your value and embracing your unique talents. As you nurture your self-worth, you'll find it easier to make bold financial decisions and seize opportunities.

Staying Open to Opportunities

The wealth mindset embraces change and welcomes opportunities. Be open to trying new things, learning from failures, and adjusting your course as needed. A fixed mindset sees challenges as roadblocks, while a growth mindset views them as stepping stones toward greater understanding and success.

Action Steps for Cultivating a Wealth Mindset

1. **Awareness**: Recognize any limiting beliefs you hold about money and success.

2. **Affirmations**: Create positive affirmations that counter these limiting beliefs.

3. **Gratitude Practice**: Dedicate time daily to express gratitude for your current financial state.

4. **Visualization**: Spend a few minutes each day visualizing your financial goals as achieved.

5. **Surround Yourself**: Engage with individuals who have a positive mindset toward wealth creation.

6. **Learning**: Continuously educate yourself about financial principles and personal growth.

7. **Take Inspired Action**: Apply your newfound beliefs to take courageous steps toward your goals.

Conclusion: Harnessing the Power Within

As we conclude this chapter, remember that your mindset is the foundation upon which your financial success is built. Cultivating a wealth mindset empowers you to see opportunities where others see challenges, and to embrace the journey toward prosperity with confidence and determination. With the keys to the wealth mindset in your hands, you are ready to unlock the doors to abundance that await you in the pages that follow.

In Chapter 2, we'll delve into the practical application of your skills to create tangible income streams that propel you closer to your financial aspirations. The journey has just begun, and your path to wealth is brightly illuminated by your newfound mindset.

Chapter 1 Exercises: Cultivating a Wealth Mindset

Exercise 1: Reflecting on Your Current Mindset

Take a few moments to reflect on your current mindset about money and wealth. Are there any limiting beliefs or negative thought patterns that come to mind? Write them down. Then, challenge each belief by reframing it in a positive and empowering way. For example, if you find yourself thinking, "I'll never be rich," reframe it as, "I am capable of attracting wealth through my skills and efforts."

Exercise 2: Visualization for Abundance

Find a quiet space where you won't be disturbed. Close your eyes and take a few deep breaths. Visualize yourself in a state of financial abundance. Imagine the lifestyle you desire, the experiences you want to have, and the impact you want to make. Engage all your senses to make the visualization as vivid as possible. Spend at least 5-10 minutes in this visualization every day for the next week.

Exercise 3: Gratitude Journaling

Start a gratitude journal specifically focused on your financial journey. Each day, write down at least three things related to money that you're grateful for. These could be small wins, unexpected opportunities, or simply the resources you have available to you. Practicing gratitude can shift your focus from scarcity to abundance.

Exercise 4: Affirmations for Wealth

Create a list of positive affirmations related to wealth and abundance. These affirmations should reflect your desired money mindset. For example, "I am open to receiving abundance," "I attract financial opportunities effortlessly," or "I deserve to be prosperous." Repeat these affirmations daily, either in the morning or before going to bed.

Exercise 5: Identifying Financial Role Models

Research and identify individuals who embody the wealth mindset you aspire to cultivate. These could be entrepreneurs, investors, authors, or public figures. Study their stories and the principles they emphasize. Write down key lessons you can apply to your own journey toward financial empowerment.

Chapter 2: Leveraging Your Skills

Welcome to Chapter 2 of "Wealth Magnet." In this chapter, we embark on a journey of self-discovery and transformation as we explore the art of leveraging your unique skills for financial gain. Imagine the satisfaction of turning your passions and talents into income streams that not only support your livelihood but also align with your deepest aspirations. Let's delve into the world of skill monetization and discover how to unlock the potential within you.

Unveiling Your Unique Skills

At the core of every individual lies a treasure trove of skills, talents, and passions waiting to be unearthed. Whether you're a wordsmith, an artist, a coder, or a problem solver, your unique abilities are the foundation of your financial journey. Start by taking an inventory of your skills. What do you excel at? What activities bring you joy and fulfillment? These are the talents that will become the building blocks of your income streams.

From Passion to Profit

Monetizing your skills isn't about turning your passions into soulless tasks; it's about nurturing your passions while making a living. If you love writing, explore freelance writing opportunities. If you're an artist, consider selling your artwork. Embrace the idea that your passions can fuel your financial success.

The Power of Personal Branding

In a world driven by online presence, personal branding becomes paramount. Establishing a personal brand helps you stand out in a crowded marketplace. Use social media, blogs, and other platforms to showcase your expertise and connect with your target audience. Share valuable insights, offer solutions, and cultivate a community that resonates with your message.

Turning Skills into Services

Your skills can manifest as services that provide value to others. If you're an excellent photographer, offer photography sessions for special events. If you're a skilled graphic designer, create visually appealing marketing materials for businesses. Think about how your skills can solve problems for others and offer solutions.

Monetizing Online Platforms

The digital age has opened doors to a plethora of online platforms where you can leverage your skills. Freelancing websites, content creation platforms, and online marketplaces provide opportunities to connect with clients and customers globally. The ability to work remotely and reach a vast audience can significantly amplify your income potential.

Balancing Passion and Profit

While monetizing your skills is empowering, it's essential to strike a balance between passion and profit. Pursue opportunities that align with your passions, but also assess their financial viability. Sometimes, making minor adjustments to your approach can transform a hobby into a lucrative venture.

Action Steps to Leverage Your Skills

1. **Self-Discovery**: Identify your top skills and passions.

2. **Market Research**: Research the demand and potential income for your chosen skill.

3. **Set Goals**: Define your income goals and the timeframe for achieving them.

4. **Skill Enhancement**: Continuously improve your skills to stay competitive.

5. **Build a Portfolio**: Create a portfolio showcasing your work and expertise.

6. **Networking**: Connect with potential clients and collaborators in your field.

7. **Promotion**: Develop a personal brand and promote your skills online.

8. **Deliver Value**: Focus on delivering high-quality results to build a positive reputation.

9. **Adapt and Innovate**: Be open to adapting your approach based on feedback and trends.

Conclusion: Empowering Your Journey

With the completion of this chapter, you've embarked on a transformative journey of turning your passions and skills into tangible income streams. By recognizing your unique abilities, setting goals, and pursuing opportunities that align with your values, you're taking significant steps toward financial empowerment.

In Chapter 3, we'll delve into the world of passive income—a realm where your money works for you while you focus on other pursuits. We'll uncover the strategies that allow you to generate continuous revenue with minimal effort, creating a pathway to financial freedom. The adventure continues, and the horizon of possibilities expands with each page turned.

Chapter 2: Leveraging Your Skills Exercises

Exercise 1: Skill Assessment and Selection

Make a list of skills you possess, both professional and personal. Rank them based on your proficiency and interest. Choose one skill that you believe has the most potential for generating income and write a brief description of why you've selected it.

Exercise 2: Identifying Value Propositions

For the skill you've chosen, define the unique value you can offer to others. What problems can you solve? How can you enhance someone's life or business? Write down at least three compelling value propositions related to your chosen skill.

Exercise 3: Target Audience Exploration

Identify your potential target audience for the skill-based service or product you're considering. Research their needs, pain points, and preferences. Create a brief profile of your ideal customer and what they're looking for.

Exercise 4: Skill Monetization Strategies

Brainstorm different ways you can monetize your chosen skill. Consider options like freelancing, consulting, teaching, creating online courses, offering workshops, or providing services on platforms like Fiverr or Upwork.

Exercise 5: Developing Your Skill Marketing Plan

Create a marketing plan for promoting your skill-based service or product. Outline strategies for building your brand, reaching your target audience, and communicating your value propositions. Include both online and offline tactics.

Exercise 6: Pricing Your Skill

Research how others in your field are pricing similar services or products. Determine the value you're delivering and set a competitive yet profitable price point. Consider any additional costs, such as materials or platform fees.

Exercise 7: Skill Enhancement Goals

Set goals for improving and expanding the skill you're leveraging. Identify specific areas where you want to enhance your proficiency or learn new techniques. Break these goals into smaller milestones with measurable outcome

Chapter 3: Passive Income Blueprint

Welcome to Chapter 3 of "Wealth Magnet." In this transformative chapter, we explore the concept of passive income—an ingenious strategy that allows you to create a steady stream of revenue with minimal ongoing effort. Imagine waking up to money flowing into your account while you focus on the things you love. Let's unveil the passive income blueprint and set you on the path to financial freedom.

Decoding Passive Income

Passive income is the embodiment of the adage "work smarter, not harder." Unlike traditional active income, which requires your continuous time and effort, passive income sources generate revenue even when you're not actively involved. These income streams become your financial allies, bolstering your financial stability and enabling you to pursue your dreams.

Exploring Passive Income Streams

There's a myriad of passive income opportunities waiting to be tapped. Here are a few popular avenues to consider:

1. **Dividend Stocks**: Invest in stocks that pay dividends, allowing you to earn a portion of the company's profits regularly.

2. **Real Estate Crowdfunding**: Participate in real estate projects by investing small amounts through crowdfunding platforms.

3. **Peer-to-Peer Lending**: Lend money to individuals or small businesses through online platforms and earn interest.

4. **Royalties**: Create and sell intellectual property like books, music, or software, earning royalties each time it's used.

5. **Automated Online Businesses**: Set up an e-commerce store using dropshipping, where a third party handles inventory and shipping.

6. **Rental Properties**: Invest in real estate properties and generate income through rent payments.

Creating Your Passive Income Portfolio

Diversification is key to building a stable passive income portfolio. By investing in multiple streams, you mitigate risk and increase your chances of consistent returns. Start small, research your options thoroughly, and gradually expand your portfolio over time.

Nurturing Your Income Streams

While passive income requires less ongoing effort, it's not entirely hands-off. Regular monitoring and maintenance are essential to ensure your income streams remain healthy. Reinvesting your earnings, staying updated with market trends, and adapting to changing circumstances will safeguard your financial growth.

Setting Up Passive Income Streams

1. **Education**: Learn about different passive income opportunities and understand their risks and rewards.

2. **Research**: Study platforms and opportunities that align with your interests and financial goals.

3. **Initial Investment**: Allocate capital to start your chosen passive income venture.

4. **Implementation**: Follow step-by-step guides to set up your chosen income stream.

5. **Automation**: Utilize tools and systems to automate processes and reduce your involvement.

Action Steps for Building Passive Income

1. **Goal Setting**: Define your passive income goals and the timeframe to achieve them.

2. **Education**: Invest time in learning about different passive income options.

3. **Start Small**: Begin with a manageable investment and expand over time.

4. **Diversify**: Build a portfolio with multiple income streams to spread risk.

5. **Monitoring**: Regularly review your investments and make necessary adjustments.

6. **Reinvestment**: Reinvest earnings to accelerate your passive income growth.

7. **Adaptability**: Stay open to new opportunities and adjust strategies as needed.

Conclusion: Your Path to Financial Freedom

As we conclude this chapter, you've unlocked the door to passive income, a powerful tool that can transform your financial landscape. By creating multiple streams of revenue that work for you while you focus on other aspects of your life, you're embarking on a journey toward financial freedom and flexibility.

In Chapter 4, we'll delve into the realm of digital entrepreneurship—exploring the world of online businesses, e-commerce, and the art of making money while you sleep. Get ready to uncover the possibilities of the digital world and harness the potential to create substantial returns with minimal initial investment.

Chapter 3 Exercises: Passive Income Blueprint Exercises

Exercise 1: Clarifying Your Passive Income Goals

Take a moment to define your passive income goals. Determine how much passive income you want to generate each month or year. Consider what this income would allow you to achieve and how it aligns with your overall financial aspirations.

Exercise 2: Brainstorming Passive Income Streams

Create a list of potential passive income streams you could pursue. Think outside the box and consider a variety of sources, such as investments, digital products, rental properties, dividend stocks, or affiliate marketing.

Exercise 3: Assessing Your Resources

For each passive income idea you've brainstormed, assess the resources you currently have available—financial, time, skills, and connections. Determine which ideas are feasible given your current circumstances.

Exercise 4: Selecting Your First Passive Income Stream

Choose one passive income idea from your list that resonates with you and aligns with your resources and goals. Write a brief description of why you're excited about this idea and how you plan to get started.

Exercise 5: Developing Your Passive Income Plan

Create a step-by-step plan for launching and managing your chosen passive income stream. Outline the tasks required to set up, maintain, and grow the income source. Break down each task into smaller action items with specific deadlines.

Exercise 6: Calculating Your Break-Even Point

Determine the point at which your passive income will cover your initial investment or expenses. Calculate the expected time it will take for your passive income stream to become profitable. Use this information to set realistic expectations.

Exercise 7: Monitoring and Adjusting

Develop a system to monitor the performance of your passive income stream regularly. Identify key metrics to track, such as revenue, expenses, and growth. Plan how you will make adjustments if necessary to optimize results.

Chapter 4: Digital Entrepreneurship

Welcome to Chapter 4 of "Wealth Magnet." In this digital age, the landscape of entrepreneurship has undergone a revolutionary transformation. The power of the internet has democratized business ownership, allowing individuals like you to venture into the world of online commerce with minimal capital. Let's dive into the world of digital entrepreneurship, where innovation and determination can pave the way to substantial returns.

The New Frontier of Online Businesses

Digital entrepreneurship is the art of creating and managing online businesses that cater to a global audience. The barriers to entry are lower than ever, enabling you to turn your passion into profit from the comfort of your home. From e-commerce stores to content creation platforms, the possibilities are vast and promising.

Starting an E-Commerce Store

E-commerce has emerged as a game-changer in the business world. You can set up a virtual storefront and sell products to a worldwide audience without the need for a physical location. From dropshipping to creating your own products, e-commerce provides diverse avenues for revenue generation.

Affiliate Marketing: Selling Without Selling

Affiliate marketing is a brilliant concept that allows you to earn a commission by promoting products or services offered by other companies. When someone makes a purchase through your affiliate link, you earn a percentage of the sale. This approach lets you focus on marketing and connecting with your audience rather than dealing with inventory or customer support.

Content Creation and Monetization

If you have a talent for creating valuable content—whether it's through blogging, podcasting, or video—you can leverage your skills for income. Platforms like YouTube, podcasts, and blogs offer opportunities for ad revenue, sponsorships, and merchandise sales. Consistency, quality, and building a loyal audience are key to success in content creation.

Nurturing Your Online Presence

A strong online presence is essential for digital entrepreneurship. Invest in building a user-friendly website, optimizing your social media profiles, and crafting compelling content. Your online presence is your virtual storefront—it's where potential customers and clients first encounter your brand.

Strategies for Success

1. **Identify a Niche**: Choose a niche that aligns with your passion and expertise.

2. **Market Research**: Study your target audience and their needs.

3. **Build a Website**: Create a professional, user-friendly website for your business.

4. **Content Creation**: Develop high-quality content that provides value to your audience.

5. **Promotion**: Utilize social media, email marketing, and other channels to promote your business.

6. **SEO Optimization**: Optimize your content for search engines to increase visibility.

7. **Networking**: Connect with other entrepreneurs and potential collaborators.

8. **Adapt and Innovate**: Stay updated with industry trends and adapt your strategies.

Action Steps for Digital Entrepreneurship

1. **Passion Identification**: Identify your passion and how it can solve a problem or fulfill a need.

2. **Market Research**: Understand your target audience and their preferences.

3. **Business Model**: Choose a suitable business model (e.g., e-commerce, affiliate marketing, content creation).

4. **Create a Plan**: Develop a comprehensive business plan that outlines your goals and strategies.

5. **Platform Selection**: Choose the right online platforms to establish your presence.

6. **Content Creation**: Consistently produce high-quality content that resonates with your audience.

7. **Promotion and Marketing**: Implement effective marketing techniques to attract customers.

8. **Continuous Learning**: Stay updated with industry trends and continually improve your skills.

Conclusion: Building Your Digital Empire

As we conclude this chapter, you've ventured into the realm of digital entrepreneurship—a world of limitless possibilities and innovative ventures. By harnessing the power of the internet, you're positioned to create substantial returns with a low initial investment. The journey continues in Chapter 5, where we explore the dynamic world of real estate riches on a budget. Prepare to discover unconventional strategies that open doors to property ownership and financial growth.

Chapter 4: Digital Entrepreneurship Exercises

Exercise 1: Niche Selection

Identify a specific niche or industry that you're passionate about and interested in exploring as a digital entrepreneur. Research the market demand, competition, and potential audience size within this niche.

Exercise 2: Defining Your Value Proposition

Based on your chosen niche, define your unique value proposition. How will you stand out from competitors? What problem will your digital business solve for your target audience? Craft a clear and compelling value proposition statement.

Exercise 3: Content Creation Plan

Create a content plan for your digital business. Outline the types of content you'll produce (e.g., blog posts, videos, podcasts), the topics you'll cover, and the frequency of your content updates. This plan will serve as the foundation of your online presence.

Exercise 4: Building Your Digital Platform

Choose the digital platforms that align with your business goals, such as a website, social media profiles, and email marketing. Create a checklist of the steps required to set up and optimize each platform for your target audience.

Exercise 5: Crafting Your Brand Identity

Develop your brand identity, including your business name, logo, color scheme, and visual elements. Consider how your brand will resonate with your target audience and reflect your value proposition.

Exercise 6: Monetization Strategies

Explore different monetization strategies for your digital business. Research options such as affiliate marketing, sponsored content, online courses, e-books, digital products, or subscription services. Evaluate which strategies align best with your niche and audience.

Exercise 7: Content Calendar and Promotion Plan

Create a content calendar outlining your content topics, publication dates, and promotion strategies. Determine how you'll share your content across various platforms to reach a wider audience and attract potential customers.

Chapter 5: Real Estate Riches on a Budget

Welcome to Chapter 5 of "Wealth Magnet." The allure of real estate investment has captivated individuals for generations. However, the perception of high barriers to entry often deter aspiring investors with limited capital. In this chapter, we shatter that misconception as we explore unconventional strategies that enable you to navigate the world of real estate riches on a budget.

The Myths and Realities of Real Estate Investment

Real estate is often associated with significant investments and substantial risk. While these elements exist in the traditional real estate landscape, innovative strategies have emerged that allow you to enter the market with a modest budget. By exploring alternative paths, you can unlock the potential for substantial returns without draining your bank account.

Wholesaling: The Path of the Savvy Investor

Wholesaling is a creative approach to real estate investment that requires minimal upfront capital. In this strategy, you act as an intermediary between sellers and buyers. You secure a property under contract at a favorable price and then assign the contract to a buyer for a fee. This approach allows you to generate income without the responsibility of property ownership.

Lease Options: A Gateway to Ownership

Lease options provide an excellent opportunity for individuals who want to build equity and potentially own a property in the future. With this strategy, you lease a property with an option to buy it at a predetermined price within a specified period. Lease options allow you to control a property without the immediate financial burden of ownership.

House Hacking: Living and Earning Simultaneously

House hacking is a brilliant strategy that merges real estate investment with cost-saving living arrangements. By purchasing a multifamily property, you can live in one unit and rent out the others. The rental income from your tenants offsets your mortgage expenses, enabling you to live almost rent-free while building equity.

The Role of Creative Financing

Creative financing is the linchpin of real estate riches on a budget. Strategies like seller financing, private lending, and creative deal structuring empower you to acquire properties without relying solely on traditional bank loans. These techniques provide flexibility and open doors to properties that might be otherwise inaccessible.

Building Your Real Estate Network

Networking is vital in the real estate industry. Connect with fellow investors, real estate agents, lenders, and mentors who can guide you on your journey. Attending local real estate meetups, workshops, and online communities can provide valuable insights and opportunities for collaboration.

Action Steps for Real Estate Riches

1. **Education**: Learn about creative real estate investment strategies.

2. **Market Research**: Identify potential markets and property types that align with your goals.

3. **Networking**: Connect with local real estate professionals and investors.

4. **Identify Deals**: Scout for distressed properties, motivated sellers, and potential lease options.

5. **Financial Planning**: Assess your budget and determine your investment capacity.

6. **Creative Financing**: Explore seller financing, private lending, and other innovative financing methods.

7. **Due Diligence**: Conduct thorough research and due diligence on potential properties.

8. **Negotiation**: Negotiate favorable terms with sellers and buyers.

Conclusion: Your Path to Real Estate Success

As we conclude this chapter, you've uncovered the blueprint to real estate riches on a budget. By adopting creative strategies like wholesaling, lease options, and house hacking, you can navigate the real estate landscape with confidence, even without a substantial initial investment. In Chapter 6, we'll dive into the world of side hustles that pay—a realm of diversified income streams that can boost your financial growth. Get ready to explore a variety of ventures that harmonize with your skills and passions.

Chapter 5: Real Estate Riches on a Budget Exercises

Exercise 1: Setting Real Estate Goals

Define your real estate investment goals. Are you aiming for rental income, property appreciation, or a combination of both? Determine your desired timeline for achieving these goals and the financial milestones you want to reach.

Exercise 2: Researching Low-Cost Markets

Research real estate markets that offer affordable properties and potential for growth. Consider factors like job opportunities, population trends, and local economic conditions. Create a shortlist of markets that align with your goals.

Exercise 3: Identifying Investment Strategies

Based on your budget and goals, explore different real estate investment strategies such as fix-and-flip, rental properties, or wholesaling. Compare the pros and cons of each strategy and select the one that resonates with you.

Exercise 4: Building a Network

Start building a network of real estate professionals, including agents, brokers, contractors, and property managers. Attend local real estate meetups, workshops, and online forums to connect with experienced individuals who can offer guidance.

Exercise 5: Creating a Budget and Financing Plan

Determine how much you're willing to invest in your first real estate venture. Create a detailed budget that includes the property purchase price, renovation costs, and other expenses. Research financing options, such as mortgages or private lenders, that align with your budget.

Exercise 6: Analyzing Deals

Practice analyzing potential real estate deals. Use metrics like the 1% rule, cash-on-cash return, and cap rate to assess the profitability of properties. Evaluate different properties to develop a keen eye for spotting lucrative opportunities.

Exercise 7: Due Diligence Checklist

Develop a due diligence checklist that outlines the steps you'll take to thoroughly research a property before making a purchase. Include tasks such as property inspections, title searches, and analyzing local market trends.

Chapter 6: Side Hustles That Pay

Welcome to Chapter 6 of "Wealth Magnet." In the pursuit of financial empowerment, side hustles stand as powerful allies. These ventures not only provide additional income but also offer opportunities to explore your passions, hone your skills, and create diverse revenue streams. Let's delve into the world of side hustles that pay, where your talents become the cornerstone of your financial success.

The Power of the Side Hustle

A side hustle is a supplementary income source pursued alongside your main job or commitments. These ventures offer numerous benefits, from financial freedom to skill development. Whether you're aiming to pay off debt, save for a specific goal, or simply enhance your financial security, side hustles can be tailored to your needs and aspirations.

Turning Hobbies into Income Streams

Do you have a hobby that brings you joy? Transforming your hobbies into side hustles can be both fulfilling and profitable. Whether you're passionate about photography, crafting, baking, or gardening, there's potential to monetize your talents and share your creations with a wider audience.

Tutoring and Online Education

If you possess expertise in a particular subject or skill, consider offering tutoring services. Whether it's academic subjects, musical instruments, or foreign languages, there's a demand for knowledge. You can also venture into online education by creating courses or tutorials on platforms like Udemy or Teachable.

Freelancing and Consulting

Your professional skills can be turned into profitable ventures through freelancing and consulting. Whether you're a graphic designer, writer, marketer, or programmer, platforms like Upwork and Fiverr offer a marketplace for your services. Consulting in your area of expertise can also be lucrative, whether you advise individuals, small businesses, or startups.

Delivery and Rideshare Services

In the era of gig economy, delivery and rideshare services offer flexible earning opportunities. If you have a reliable vehicle and enjoy driving, platforms like Uber, Lyft, and food delivery services allow you to earn extra income on your own schedule.

Balancing Act: Side Hustles and Full-Time Jobs

While side hustles are exciting avenues for additional income, maintaining a healthy work-life balance is crucial. Ensure that your side hustle commitments do not overwhelm your main job or personal life. Time management and prioritization become your allies as you navigate the dual responsibilities.

Strategies for Success

1. **Skill Assessment**: Identify your skills and passions that can be monetized.

2. **Market Research**: Identify the demand and potential income for your chosen side hustle.

3. **Platform Selection**: Choose the right platforms for offering your services or products.

4. **Pricing**: Set competitive and reasonable prices for your offerings.

5. **Marketing**: Promote your side hustle through social media, word of mouth, and online platforms.

6. **Time Management**: Create a schedule that allows you to balance your main job, side hustle, and personal life.

7. **Quality Control**: Deliver high-quality products or services to build a positive reputation.

Action Steps for Launching a Side Hustle

1. **Passion Identification**: Determine your strengths and areas of expertise.

2. **Market Research**: Research the demand and competition for your chosen side hustle.

3. **Business Plan**: Create a plan outlining your offerings, target audience, and pricing strategy.

4. **Set Up**: Establish your online presence, whether through a website, social media, or platforms.

5. **Launch**: Launch your side hustle and start promoting your offerings.

6. **Network**: Connect with potential clients or customers and build relationships.

7. **Consistency**: Stay consistent in delivering quality products or services.

Conclusion: Your Gateway to Financial Growth

As we conclude this chapter, you've ventured into the world of side hustles—a realm of opportunity where your skills, passions, and ambitions converge to create additional income streams. By embracing side hustles that resonate with you, you're well on your way to enhancing your financial growth and achieving your goals.

In Chapter 7, we'll explore the philosophy of frugal living—a practice that amplifies your savings and accelerates your path to financial independence. Get ready to unlock the secrets of smart spending and discover how living intentionally can pave the way to financial abundance.

Chapter 6 Exercises: Side Hustles That Pay

Exercise 1: Identifying Your Passion Projects

Take some time to reflect on your passions and interests outside of your main occupation. Write down at least three activities or hobbies that bring you joy and fulfillment. These will serve as a starting point for potential side hustles.

Exercise 2: Researching Market Demand

Choose one of the passion projects you've identified and research the market demand for related products or services. Look into competitors, target audience preferences, and potential gaps you can fill with your unique offerings.

Exercise 3: Brainstorming Income-Generating Ideas

Based on your research, brainstorm different ways you can turn your passion project into a side hustle that generates income. Consider various formats such as physical products, digital services, workshops, or online courses.

Exercise 4: Evaluating Feasibility

Select one of the side hustle ideas you've brainstormed and evaluate its feasibility. Assess factors such as initial investment, time commitment, required skills, and potential returns. This exercise will help you choose a side hustle that aligns with your resources and goals.

Exercise 5: Creating a Side Hustle Plan

Develop a comprehensive plan for launching and growing your chosen side hustle. Outline the steps you need to take, including product creation, marketing strategies, pricing, and distribution. Break down these steps into actionable tasks and set deadlines.

Chapter 7: The Art of Frugal Living

Welcome to Chapter 7 of "Wealth Magnet." In a world that often promotes excessive consumerism, the art of frugal living stands as a powerful counterbalance. By adopting mindful spending habits, you can amplify your savings, accelerate your financial goals, and pave the way to lasting prosperity. Let's delve into the philosophy of frugality and unlock the secrets to living intentionally.

Redefining Your Relationship with Money

Frugal living is not about depriving yourself or sacrificing your quality of life. It's about making conscious choices that align with your values and financial aspirations. By redefining your relationship with money, you gain greater control over your financial destiny.

Intentional Spending: Quality Over Quantity

Intentional spending is at the heart of frugal living. Instead of mindlessly purchasing items, evaluate each expense based on its value and impact on your life. Prioritize purchases that enhance your well-being, support your goals, and align with your values.

Cutting Unnecessary Expenses

Analyze your monthly expenses and identify areas where you can cut back without compromising your happiness. This might involve reducing dining out, canceling unused subscriptions, or finding more cost-effective alternatives for everyday expenses.

Embracing Minimalism

Minimalism is a lifestyle that focuses on decluttering your physical and mental spaces. By reducing excess belongings, you not only free up physical space but also cultivate a sense of contentment that isn't reliant on material possessions.

DIY and Self-Sufficiency

Embracing DIY (Do It Yourself) projects and self-sufficiency can significantly reduce costs. Whether it's cooking meals at home, repairing items, or growing your own produce, these skills empower you to rely less on external services and products.

The Joy of Savings and Investment

Frugality isn't just about cutting expenses—it's about channeling the savings into opportunities that yield long-term benefits. Allocate the money you save toward investments, savings accounts, or debt reduction. Witnessing your savings grow is an empowering motivator on your financial journey.

Strategies for Successful Frugal Living

1. **Budgeting**: Create a detailed budget that outlines your income, expenses, and savings goals.

2. **Expense Tracking**: Monitor your spending to identify areas where you can cut back.

3. **Prioritization**: Prioritize expenses that align with your values and long-term goals.

4. **Mindful Shopping**: Practice mindful shopping by evaluating each purchase's value.

5. **Homemade and DIY**: Explore DIY solutions for everyday items and services.

6. **Debt Reduction**: Allocate saved funds toward paying off debts faster.

7. **Investment**: Invest your savings into vehicles that generate passive income or appreciate over time.

Action Steps for Embracing Frugality

1. **Assessment**: Analyze your current spending habits and identify areas for improvement.

2. **Budget Creation**: Develop a realistic budget that accounts for your income and expenses.

3. **Cut Back:**Identify unnecessary expenses and find ways to cut back.

4. **Mindful Spending**: Before making a purchase, ask yourself if it aligns with your values.

5. **DIY Exploration**: Explore DIY projects for items you frequently purchase.

6. **Savings Plan**: Set up a dedicated savings account for your frugal living goals.

7. **Regular Evaluation**: Regularly review your budget and expenses to ensure you're on track.

Conclusion: Cultivating Financial Freedom

As we conclude this chapter, you've delved into the art of frugal living—a practice that empowers you to live intentionally, make conscious choices, and amplify your savings. By aligning your spending habits with your values and aspirations, you're embracing the path to financial freedom and setting the stage for lasting prosperity.

In Chapter 8, we'll explore the power of networking—a dynamic strategy that connects you with valuable relationships, collaborations, and opportunities. Get ready to unlock the potential of networking and harness the collective wisdom that propels your financial journey.

Chapter 7 Exercises: The Art of Frugal Living

Exercise 1: Tracking Your Expenses

For the next month, track all of your expenses, both big and small. Use a notebook, spreadsheet, or a budgeting app to record each expenditure. At the end of the month, review your spending patterns and identify areas where you can potentially cut back.

Exercise 2: Identifying Wants vs. Needs

Go through your list of expenses and categorize them into "wants" and "needs." Consider whether each expense is essential for your well-being or simply a desire. Reflect on how your spending aligns with your financial goals.

Exercise 3: Implementing the 24-Hour Rule

Practice the "24-hour rule" before making any non-essential purchases. When you're tempted to buy something, wait for 24 hours before making the decision. Use this time to consider whether the purchase is truly aligned with your priorities and values.

Exercise 4: Decluttering and Selling Unused Items

Take a day to declutter your living space and identify items you no longer use or need. Consider selling these items online or through a garage sale. Use the proceeds to bolster your savings or invest in income-generating opportunities.

Exercise 5: Creating a Frugal Challenge

Challenge yourself to a week of frugal living. Set a budget for your discretionary spending (e.g., eating out, entertainment) and stick to it. Find creative and cost-effective ways to enjoy your week without overspending.

Chapter 8: The Power of Networking

Welcome to Chapter 8 of "Wealth Magnet." In the interconnected world we live in, networking has emerged as a formidable catalyst for success. The power of building meaningful relationships, forging collaborations, and tapping into a network's collective wisdom can propel you toward financial abundance. Let's explore the art of networking and uncover how it can be harnessed to unlock new opportunities and elevate your financial journey.

The Network Effect: Amplifying Your Reach

The network effect is a phenomenon where the value of a network increases as more people join it. By connecting with diverse individuals, you amplify your reach, expose yourself to different perspectives, and gain access to a wealth of knowledge and opportunities.

Building Authentic Relationships

Networking is not about transactional exchanges—it's about forming authentic relationships. Approach networking with a genuine desire to connect, learn from others, and contribute to their success. Authenticity fosters trust and lays the foundation for long-lasting collaborations.

Expanding Your Horizons

Networking introduces you to individuals from varied backgrounds, industries, and experiences. Engaging with people who think differently can spark innovative ideas, broaden your horizons, and challenge your assumptions. Embrace the diversity within your network to stimulate your own growth.

The Collaborative Advantage

Collaborations are a hallmark of effective networking. By partnering with others, you can pool resources, skills, and knowledge to achieve shared goals. Collaborative projects can lead to new ventures, increased visibility, and mutually beneficial outcomes.

Leveraging Online Platforms

The digital era has revolutionized networking, offering platforms to connect with individuals globally. Social media, online communities, and professional networking sites provide opportunities to engage, share insights, and build relationships from the comfort of your own space.

Networking Events and Conferences

Attending networking events, workshops, and conferences can provide unparalleled opportunities to connect face-to-face with like-minded individuals. These gatherings offer a fertile ground for learning, collaboration, and establishing meaningful connections.

Strategies for Successful Networking

1. **Value Exchange**: Approach networking with a mindset of giving before receiving.

2. **Active Listening**: Listen attentively to others, show genuine interest, and ask thoughtful questions.

3. **Reciprocity**: Offer your help and support to others, fostering a culture of reciprocity.

4. **Diversification**: Engage with individuals from diverse backgrounds and industries.

5. **Online Engagement**: Participate in online discussions, forums, and social media groups.

6. **Face-to-Face Interactions**: Attend networking events and conferences to connect in person.

Action Steps for Effective Networking

1. **Networking Goals**: Define your networking objectives and what you hope to achieve.

2. **Research**: Identify relevant networking events, groups, and online platforms.

3. **Engagement**: Participate actively in discussions, share insights, and contribute value.

4. **Follow-Up**: After connecting, follow up with individuals to nurture relationships.

5. **Long-Term Relationships**: Cultivate authentic relationships over time, beyond one-time interactions.

6. **Give and Receive**: Offer your expertise and support while also seeking guidance and collaboration.

Conclusion: Your Network, Your Wealth

As we conclude this chapter, you've unlocked the power of networking—a dynamic force that can connect you with valuable relationships, collaborations, and opportunities. By nurturing authentic connections and embracing the collective wisdom of your network, you're harnessing a powerful tool that accelerates your financial journey and propels you toward lasting success.

In the final chapter, Chapter 9, we'll bring together all the key lessons and insights you've gained throughout this book. You'll embark on a reflective journey to synthesize your newfound knowledge and create a personalized roadmap for your financial growth.

Chapter 8: The Power of Networking Exercises

Exercise 1: Defining Your Networking Goals

Set clear networking goals for yourself. Are you seeking new business opportunities, mentorship, partnerships, or industry insights? Write down your goals to help you stay focused and intentional in your networking efforts.

Exercise 2: Identifying Your Network

Create a list of people you already know who could be part of your professional network—colleagues, friends, acquaintances, and mentors. Note their areas of expertise and how they might contribute to your goals.

Exercise 3: Expanding Your Network

Identify potential networking events, workshops, conferences, or online communities related to your field or interests. Choose a few upcoming opportunities to attend or join and mark them on your calendar.

Exercise 4: Crafting Your Elevator Pitch

Develop a concise and compelling elevator pitch that introduces yourself, your background, and your aspirations. Practice delivering this pitch with confidence, both in person and virtually.

Exercise 5: Nurturing Relationships

Select three individuals from your existing network and reach out to reconnect. Initiate a conversation, share updates, or express interest in their current endeavors. Strengthening existing connections can lead to valuable opportunities.

Exercise 6: Active Listening Practice

Practice active listening during networking interactions. Ask open-ended questions and truly engage in the conversation. Take notes on key points, and follow up with personalized messages to show your genuine interest.

Exercise 7: Offering Value

Identify ways you can offer value to your network contacts. Whether it's sharing resources, offering assistance, or connecting them with others, contributing to your network's success fosters meaningful relationships.

Chapter 9: Mastering Mindful Investing

Welcome to Chapter 9 of "Wealth Magnet." As we near the culmination of your journey toward financial empowerment, we explore the pinnacle of money mastery—mindful investing. Armed with the wisdom gained from previous chapters, you're poised to navigate the world of investments with clarity, purpose, and confidence. Let's delve into the art of mindful investing and equip you with the tools to make informed decisions that propel your financial growth.

The Essence of Mindful Investing

Mindful investing is rooted in purposeful decision-making, diligent research, and a deep understanding of risk and reward. It's about aligning your investments with your financial goals, values, and risk tolerance. By embracing a holistic approach to investing, you can capitalize on opportunities while safeguarding your financial well-being.

Investment Vehicles: Exploring Options

From stocks and bonds to real estate and mutual funds, a myriad of investment vehicles beckon. Each comes with its own set of risks and potential returns. The key is to select investments that resonate with your long-term objectives and align with your risk profile.

Diversification: The Pillar of Risk Management

Diversification is the strategy of spreading your investments across various assets to reduce risk. By diversifying your portfolio, you can minimize the impact of volatility in any single investment. Balancing high-risk, high-reward options with more stable investments ensures stability while allowing for growth.

Research and Due Diligence

In the realm of mindful investing, thorough research is paramount. Investigate potential investments, analyze market trends, and understand the underlying factors that drive returns. Avoid impulsive decisions and make choices based on solid information.

Understanding Risk and Reward

Every investment carries a degree of risk, and assessing risk is crucial to informed decision-making. Evaluate the potential rewards against the associated risks. As a mindful investor, you'll learn to strike a balance that aligns with your financial objectives and comfort level.

The Long View: Patience and Discipline

Mindful investing embraces a long-term perspective. Avoid chasing quick gains and focus on sustainable growth. Patience and discipline are your allies as you ride out market fluctuations, allowing your investments to mature over time.

Strategies for Mindful Investing

1. **Goal Alignment**: Define your financial goals and tailor your investments to achieve them.

2. **Risk Assessment**: Understand your risk tolerance and choose investments accordingly.

3. **Diversification**: Spread your investments across different asset classes.

4. **Research**: Thoroughly research and analyze potential investment opportunities.

5. **Long-Term Vision**: Embrace a long-term perspective, avoiding reactionary decisions.

6. **Regular Review**: Periodically assess and adjust your investment portfolio.

7. **Professional Advice**: Seek guidance from financial advisors and experts.

Action Steps for Mindful Investing

1. **Goal Definition**: Define your short-term and long-term financial goals.

2. **Risk Assessment**: Determine your risk tolerance and comfort with potential losses.

3. **Asset Allocation**: Allocate your investments across different asset classes.

4. **Research Plan**: Develop a plan for researching potential investment opportunities.

5. **Diversification** Strategy: Create a diversified portfolio that balances risk and reward.

6. **Patience and Monitoring**: Commit to long-term investing while regularly monitoring your portfolio.

7. **Expert Consultation**: Consider seeking advice from financial advisors or experts.

Conclusion: Your Path to Financial Mastery

As we conclude this chapter, you've embarked on the final phase of your financial journey—mindful investing. By approaching investments with purpose, research, and a long-term perspective, you're poised to navigate the complex landscape of financial markets with confidence. With the combined knowledge from each chapter, you've created a comprehensive roadmap for your financial growth and empowerment.

Your journey doesn't end here—it's a continuous evolution. As you master the art of mindful investing, remember that every choice you make is a step toward your financial destiny. May your path be illuminated with knowledge, insight, and abundance.

Chapter 9: Mastering Mindful Investing Exercises

Exercise 1: Setting Investment Intentions

Reflect on your investment intentions. Are you aiming for long-term growth, income generation, or a balance of both? Write down your intentions and the reasons behind your investment goals.

Exercise 2: Understanding Risk Tolerance

Assess your risk tolerance level by considering how comfortable you are with potential fluctuations in your investment portfolio. Use a risk tolerance questionnaire or tool to determine your risk profile.

Exercise 3: Diversification Strategy

Evaluate your current investment portfolio, if you have one. Determine if your investments are adequately diversified across different asset classes and industries. Identify any areas where you might need to rebalance.

Exercise 4: Conducting Investment Research

Select an investment opportunity you're considering and research it thoroughly. Gather information on historical performance, market trends, and potential risks. Present your findings to a friend or family member to practice articulating your investment rationale.

Exercise 5: Embracing Patience and Long-Term Vision

Write a letter to your future self, describing your investment goals and vision. Explain why you believe in your investment strategy and the positive impact it will have on your financial future. Revisit this letter periodically to reinforce your long-term perspective.

Exercise 6: Practicing Mindful Investing

Incorporate mindfulness techniques into your investment decisions. Before making a significant investment choice, take a moment to breathe, reflect, and consider the alignment of the opportunity with your overall financial goals.

Exercise 7: Tracking Progress and Adjusting

Create a system to regularly track the performance of your investments. Set aside time each month to review your portfolio and assess whether any adjustments are necessary based on changing market conditions or your goals.

Chapter 10: Mapping Your Financial Future

Welcome to the final chapter of "Wealth Magnet." You've embarked on a transformative journey, exploring key money secrets, strategies, and insights that empower you to shape your financial destiny. As we wrap up this enlightening odyssey, it's time to synthesize your newfound knowledge and chart a course that propels you toward a future of abundance, freedom, and prosperity. Let's dive into the process of mapping your financial future and creating a personalized roadmap for your success.

Reflecting on Your Journey

Take a moment to reflect on the knowledge you've acquired throughout this book. From cultivating a wealth mindset to harnessing the power of networking and mastering mindful investing, each chapter has equipped you with tools for financial empowerment.

Defining Your Vision

Start by defining your vision for the future. Envision your desired financial state—whether it's achieving debt freedom, owning a home, traveling the world, or retiring comfortably. Your vision will serve as your compass, guiding your decisions and actions.

Setting Clear Goals

Break down your vision into actionable goals. Make them specific, measurable, achievable, relevant, and time-bound (SMART). Whether it's saving a certain amount, starting a business, or paying off debt, clear goals provide a roadmap for your journey.

Creating a Personalized Roadmap

With your goals in mind, create a roadmap that outlines the steps you'll take to achieve them. Consider the strategies you've learned in each chapter and how they apply to your unique situation. Your roadmap should encompass budgeting, saving, investing, and exploring income opportunities.

Adapting and Course Correcting

Flexibility is key on your financial journey. Life is dynamic, and circumstances may change. Regularly review your goals and roadmap, and be open to adjusting them as needed. Embrace change as an opportunity to fine-tune your path.

Celebrating Milestones

Celebrate your achievements along the way, no matter how small. Every step forward brings you closer to your financial goals. Acknowledge your progress and use it as motivation to continue pushing forward.

Continued Learning and Growth

Your journey doesn't end with this book. Commit to continued learning and personal growth. Stay informed about financial trends, explore new opportunities, and consistently enhance your financial knowledge.

Gratitude and Abundance Mindset

Practice gratitude for the progress you make. Cultivate an abundance mindset that focuses on what you have and what's possible. Embrace positivity and attract more opportunities into your life.

Your Financial Legacy

As you map your financial future, consider the legacy you want to leave. Whether it's providing for your family, supporting causes you're passionate about, or inspiring others, your financial success can have a profound impact beyond yourself.

Taking the Next Steps

1. **Review Your Journey**: Reflect on the knowledge you've gained throughout this book.

2. **Define Your Vision**: Envision your desired financial future and set clear goals.

3. **Create Your Roadmap**: Outline actionable steps for achieving your goals.

4. **Stay Adaptable**: Be open to adjusting your roadmap as circumstances change.

5. **Celebrate Progress**: Acknowledge and celebrate your achievements along the way.

6. **Continued Learning**: Commit to ongoing learning and personal growth.

7. **Practice Gratitude**: Cultivate an abundance mindset and practice gratitude.

8. **Embrace Your Legacy**: Consider the impact you want to leave through your financial success.

Conclusion: Your Journey Continues

As we conclude "Wealth Magnet," remember that your journey toward financial empowerment is an ongoing evolution. By integrating the wisdom from this book and mapping your financial future, you're taking a monumental step toward the life of abundance, freedom, and prosperity you deserve.

May your path be illuminated with the brilliance of your dreams, the power of your actions, and the unwavering belief in your potential. The pages of your financial story await your pen, ready to be filled with the chapters of your accomplishments and the legacy you leave for generations to come

Chapter 10: Mapping Your Financial Future Exercises
Exercise 1: Defining Your Ideal Financial Scenario

Imagine your ideal financial future. Where do you see yourself in terms of income, assets, lifestyle, and philanthropic efforts? Write a detailed description of this vision to serve as a guide for your financial planning.

Exercise 2: Creating a Financial Vision Board

Gather images, quotes, and symbols that represent your financial goals and aspirations. Create a physical or digital vision board that visually captures your financial dreams. Display it somewhere you'll see it daily.

Exercise 3: Setting Specific Financial Milestones

Break down your long-term financial vision into specific, achievable milestones. These could be related to paying off debts, saving for a major purchase, or reaching a certain level of passive income. Write down each milestone and the date you aim to achieve it.

Exercise 4: Crafting Your Financial Plan

Develop a comprehensive financial plan that outlines your goals, strategies, and action steps for each milestone. Include details on how you'll allocate your resources, manage debt, invest, and track progress.

Exercise 5: Identifying Potential Roadblocks

Identify potential obstacles that could hinder your progress toward your financial goals. These might include unexpected expenses, market downturns, or changes in your personal circumstances. Plan how you'll navigate these challenges.

Exercise 6: Regular Financial Check-Ins

Schedule regular check-ins with yourself to review your financial plan and assess your progress. Use these moments to celebrate your successes, make adjustments if needed, and ensure you're staying on track.

Exercise 7: Sharing Your Vision

Share your financial vision and goals with a trusted friend, family member, or mentor. Discussing your aspirations with someone supportive can provide accountability and fresh perspectives on your journey.

Conclusion: Your Path to Abundance

Congratulations, dear reader, for embarking on a transformative journey through the pages of "Wealth Magnet." You've uncovered a treasure trove of key money secrets, empowering strategies, and timeless wisdom that have equipped you to forge a path to financial empowerment. As we bid farewell to this chapter of your life, let's reflect on the transformative journey you've undertaken and the boundless possibilities that lie ahead.

Your Evolution as a Wealth Magnet

From the very first chapter, you committed to evolving your mindset—a powerful shift that set the tone for your journey. You embraced the truth that wealth begins within, and that a wealth mindset serves as the foundation upon which prosperity is built. With a clear vision, you shattered limiting beliefs and stepped into the role of a true wealth magnet.

Strategies That Propel Your Prosperity

Each chapter unveiled a new facet of financial empowerment. You explored the advantages of passive income, the power of leveraging your skills, and the magic of side hustles that pay. You delved into frugal living, the art of networking, and the intricacies of mindful investing. Armed with knowledge and insight, you wielded these strategies like tools to shape your financial destiny.

Your Unique Journey: Unveiling Your Path

As you navigated this journey, you weren't just following a prescribed formula—you were uncovering your unique path. Your aspirations, values, and circumstances all played a role in shaping your financial roadmap. Through conscious decisions and deliberate actions, you forged a path that resonates with your true self and aligns with your vision of abundance.

A Continual Evolution

Remember, this is not the end; it's a new beginning. The wisdom you've gained in "Wealth Magnet" is a foundation upon which to build and expand. Your journey toward financial empowerment is an ongoing evolution, marked by continuous learning, adaptation, and growth. As you encounter new challenges and opportunities, you'll be equipped with the tools to conquer and thrive.

The Legacy You Create

The legacy you're creating extends beyond numbers on a balance sheet. It encompasses the impact you make on your life, the lives of your loved ones, and the world around you. Your pursuit of financial empowerment isn't just about personal gain—it's about embracing the responsibility to contribute positively to your community and leave a lasting legacy of abundance and inspiration.

With Gratitude and Optimism

As you close the final pages of "Wealth Magnet," do so with a heart full of gratitude and optimism. You've taken a profound step toward financial abundance, empowerment, and a life of purpose. The journey you've embarked upon is a testament to your commitment, determination, and belief in your potential to shape your own destiny.

May your days be filled with prosperity, your nights with dreams turned into reality, and your heart with the knowledge that you are the architect of your financial future. The world is ready to witness the brilliance you bring forth as you radiate the essence of a true wealth magnet.

Conclusion: Your Path to Abundance Exercises

Exercise 1: Reflecting on Your Journey

Take a moment to reflect on the insights, strategies, and exercises you've encountered throughout the book. Write a journal entry summarizing the most impactful lessons you've learned and how they've shifted your perspective on wealth and abundance.

Exercise 2: Crafting Your Personal Mantra

Create a personal mantra that encapsulates your newfound understanding of wealth and abundance. Use positive and empowering language to affirm your commitment to attracting opportunities, leveraging your skills, and pursuing financial success.

Exercise 3: Setting Actionable Intentions

Write down three actionable intentions you'll carry forward from this book. These could be related to adopting a wealth mindset, pursuing passive income opportunities, networking more effectively, or any other key concept covered in the book.

Exercise 4: Sharing Your Insights

Consider sharing your insights from the book with a friend, family member, or online community. Write a post, create a video, or host a discussion about the most valuable takeaways you've gained and how you plan to implement them in your life.

Exercise 5: Crafting a 1-Year Vision

Imagine where you want to be financially one year from now. Write a letter to yourself detailing your accomplishments, growth, and the progress you've made toward your financial goals. Seal the letter and open it in a year to celebrate your achievements.

Exercise 6: Cultivating Gratitude

Practice daily gratitude by writing down at least three things you're grateful for in your financial journey. Regularly acknowledge the progress you're making, the opportunities you're pursuing, and the abundance already present in your life.

Exercise 7: Continuous Learning and Action

Commit to continuous learning and action in your pursuit of abundance. Set a goal to read at least one new finance or self-improvement book every quarter and to take consistent steps toward your financial aspirations.

Dear Reader,

As we reach the end of this incredible journey through "Wealth Magnet," I wanted to take a moment to express my heartfelt gratitude. Your dedication to learning, growing, and embracing the wisdom within these pages has been truly inspiring.

Remember that the power to create a life of abundance, purpose, and prosperity resides within you. You have the ability to shape your financial future and leave a lasting impact on the world around you.

As you step forward on your path, know that you're not alone. The insights shared in this book will continue to accompany you, guiding you through challenges and celebrating your victories.

Your journey toward financial empowerment is a testament to your strength and resilience. Embrace every opportunity, challenge limiting beliefs, and continue to pursue knowledge and growth.

Thank you for sharing this voyage with me. I look forward to hearing about the remarkable chapters you'll write in your financial story.

With admiration and warmest wishes,

Mavin Murithi

Contact Us

We're thrilled that you're considering reaching out to us. Whether you have questions, feedback, or simply want to share your journey through "Wealth Magnet: Unlocking Key Money Secrets for Low-Capital, High-Return Success," we're here to listen and support you.

Feedback and Questions

If you have questions about the book, would like to request more information, or need assistance with any aspect of your financial journey, please feel free to contact us. Your insights and inquiries are invaluable, and we're committed to providing you with the information you need.

Sharing Your Success

We would be delighted to hear about the progress you've made by applying the strategies and insights from "Wealth Magnet." Your successes, big or small, inspire us and the entire community. Feel free to share your story, milestones, and achievements with us.

Join the Community

Connect with us and fellow readers by joining the "Wealth Magnet" community. Share your insights, engage in discussions, and be part of a community dedicated to financial empowerment and growth.

How to Reach Us

You can reach out to us through the following channels:

- **Email**: [mavinmagmt@email.com]

- **Social Media**: Connect with us on [@mavinmagmt on Instagram], where we regularly share updates, insights, and engage with our community.

- **WhatsApp**: +255629295231

We're excited to hear from you and be a part of your journey toward financial abundance, purpose, and prosperity.

Recommended Resources

As you continue your journey toward financial empowerment and growth, these resources can provide additional insights, knowledge, and inspiration to enhance your understanding and implementation of the strategies discussed in "Wealth Magnet."

Books

1. "Rich Dad Poor Dad" by Robert T. Kiyosaki

2. "The Millionaire Next Door" by Thomas J. Stanley and William D. Danko

3. "The Power of Habit" by Charles Duhigg

4. "The 4-Hour Workweek" by Timothy Ferriss

5. "The Automatic Millionaire" by David Bach

Websites and Blogs

1. **Investopedia**: An invaluable resource for understanding financial terms, concepts, and investment strategies.

2. **BiggerPockets**: A platform for real estate enthusiasts, offering advice, forums, and educational content.

3. **Mr. Money Mustache**: A blog focused on achieving financial independence and retiring early.

4. **SideHustleNation**: An online community that provides ideas, tips, and inspiration for launching and growing side hustles.

5. **LinkedIn**: A professional networking platform where you can connect with industry experts, mentors, and peers.

Podcasts

1. **The Dave Ramsey Show**: Offers practical advice on budgeting, debt reduction, and achieving financial goals.

2. **ChooseFI**: Explores the path to financial independence and provides actionable strategies for listeners.

3. **The BiggerPockets** Money Podcast: Discusses personal finance and real estate investment with expert guests.

4. **Afford Anything**: Host Paula Pant delves into money, investing, and achieving financial freedom.

5. **The Side Hustle School**: Shares real stories of individuals who have successfully started and grown side businesses.

Online Courses and Workshops

1. **Udemy**: Offers a wide range of courses on personal finance, investing, and entrepreneurship.

2. **Coursera**: Provides access to courses from top universities and institutions on financial literacy and investment strategies.

3. **Skillshare**: Features classes on entrepreneurship, freelancing, and creative ways to generate income.

These resources can serve as valuable companions on your journey to financial empowerment. Explore and engage with them to deepen your knowledge, refine your strategies, and continue your evolution toward a life of abundance and prosperity.

Glossary

Abundance Mindset: A positive belief system that focuses on the limitless possibilities for success, wealth, and opportunities.

Asset Allocation: The distribution of investments across various asset classes, such as stocks, bonds, and real estate, to manage risk and optimize returns.

Diversification: Spreading investments across different types of assets or sectors to reduce risk and increase the potential for returns.

Financial Independence: Achieving a state where your investments and passive income cover your living expenses, allowing you to choose when and how you work.

Frugal Living: Embracing a lifestyle characterized by conscious spending, prioritizing needs over wants, and minimizing unnecessary expenses.

Leveraging: Utilizing resources, skills, or assets to magnify your impact and achieve greater results.

Mindful Investing: Approaching investments with purpose, research, and a deep understanding of risk and reward.

Passive Income: Earnings generated with minimal ongoing effort, such as rental income, dividends, or royalties.

Risk Tolerance: The level of risk an individual is comfortable taking on when making investment decisions.

Side Hustle: A part-time job, project, or business pursued in addition to one's primary source of income.

Wealth Mindset: A mindset that embraces the belief in one's ability to attract and create wealth through positive thoughts and actions.

Frequently Asked Questions
1. What is a wealth mindset, and how can I develop it?
A wealth mindset is a positive attitude and belief system that empowers you to attract and create financial success. It involves cultivating thoughts, behaviors, and habits that align with abundance rather than scarcity. To develop a wealth mindset, practice gratitude, affirmations, visualization, and self-awareness exercises.
2. Can I really generate passive income with low capital?
Yes, absolutely! Many passive income opportunities require minimal upfront investment. By leveraging your skills, exploring side hustles, investing in digital assets, and starting small in real estate, you can generate passive income streams that grow over time.
3. How can I effectively network, especially if I'm an introvert?
Networking can be daunting, but it's accessible to introverts as well. Start by attending smaller events, engaging in one-on-one conversations, and focusing on genuine connections. Listen actively, ask open-ended questions, and practice active listening to build meaningful relationships.
4. What if I have limited knowledge about investing?
It's never too late to start learning about investing. Begin by educating yourself about basic investment concepts, understanding risk tolerance, and exploring low-cost investment options like index funds. Consider seeking advice from financial advisors or mentors to guide your investment decisions.
5. How do I overcome the fear of failure when starting a side hustle?
Fear of failure is common but conquerable. Embrace a growth mindset, where failures are viewed as opportunities for learning and improvement. Set realistic expectations, take calculated risks, and remember that setbacks are part of the journey toward success.
6. Can frugal living negatively impact my quality of life?

Frugal living doesn't mean sacrificing happiness; it means making intentional spending choices. Prioritize experiences over possessions, find free or low-cost activities, and focus on what truly brings joy. Frugality can lead to financial freedom without compromising on life's pleasures.

7. How do I balance my current job with building passive income streams?

Balancing a job and building passive income requires time management and dedication. Allocate specific hours for your side projects, set achievable goals, and consistently invest effort even when progress seems slow. Gradually, your passive income streams can replace or complement your job income.

8. What's the key to successful real estate investing on a budget?

Successful real estate investing on a budget involves careful research and strategic planning. Focus on affordable markets with growth potential, leverage financing options, thoroughly analyze deals, and consider creative ways to add value to properties.

9. How can I stay motivated throughout my financial journey?

Staying motivated requires continuous self-care and self-reflection. Revisit your goals regularly, celebrate small wins, seek inspiration from success stories, and remind yourself of the long-term benefits of your efforts. Engage in activities that rejuvenate your enthusiasm for your financial journey.

10. What if my financial goals change over time?

Flexibility is important on your financial journey. As your circumstances change, reassess and adjust your goals accordingly. Regularly review your financial plan, evaluate progress, and pivot when necessary to ensure your goals remain aligned with your evolving aspirations.